Praise f
Every Man's Battle

MW01037933

"There is no more common enemy of true manhood than the diversion or the perversion of our sexual capacities. I welcome every contribution to the arsenal of resistance."

—JACK W. HAYFORD, LITT.D.
pastor of the Church on the Way and
president of the King's Seminary

"This book will revolutionize the marriage of every man who reads it. Why? Because every man battles sexual temptations and every marriage grows stronger when these temptations are defeated. The vulnerable, honest, and insightful pages of this book reveal what every man must know."

—DRS. LES AND LESLIE PARROTT
authors of *Saving Your Marriage Before It Starts*

"This timely resource presents clear, practical principles for sexual purity. Arterburn and Stoeker call for courage, commitment, and self-discipline as they lead men into a more successful relationship with God, family, and spouse. This book is truly for every man."

—DR. JOHN C. MAXWELL
founder of the INJOY Group

"God has used Steve Arterburn countless times to impact my heart and life; I am thankful for him and his investment in *Every Man's Battle*. I am also grateful for Fred Stoeker. Fred pours himself into this book with honesty, vulnerability, and a practical strategy to fight the good fight. He offers biblical truth and hope to anyone with ears to hear how to battle the war of sexual temptation. Read with an open heart. *Every Man's Battle* may save your marriage and your witness."

—DR. GARY ROSBERG
president of America's Family Coaches
author of *Guard Your Heart* and *The Five Love Needs of Men and Women*

Stephen Arterburn
Fred Stoeker with Mike Yorkey

every man's battle
workbook

The Path to Sexual Integrity Starts Here

A Guide for Personal or Group Study

WATERBROOK
PRESS

EVERY MAN'S BATTLE WORKBOOK
PUBLISHED BY WATERBROOK PRESS
2375 Telstar Drive, Suite 160
Colorado Springs, Colorado 80920
A division of Random House, Inc.

Quotations from *Every Man's Battle:* © 2000 by Stephen Arterburn, Fred Stoeker,
and Mike Yorkey

All Scripture quotations, unless otherwise indicated, are taken from the *Holy Bible,
New International Version*®. NIV®. Copyright © 1973, 1978, 1984 by International
Bible Society. Used by permission of Zondervan Publishing House. All rights reserved.

Italics in Scripture quotations reflect the author's added emphasis.

The information on sexual addiction in chapter 3 is drawn from Stephen Arterburn's
Addicted to "Love" (Ann Arbor, Mich.: Vine, 1991), 109-10.

ISBN 1-57856-552-9

Published in association with the literary agency of Alive Communications, Inc.,
7680 Goddard Street, Suite 200, Colorado Springs, CO 80920.

Printed in the United States of America
2003

10 9 8 7 6 5

contents

questions you may have about this workbook

What will the *Every Man's Battle Workbook* do for me?

This workbook will guide you through some serious Bible study, an intense examination of your personal life, and an honest application of biblical truth to help you win the war on sexual temptation and live a pure life God's way.

You'll find realistic help straight from God's Word for actively training your eyes and your mind to increasingly see and think according to God's standards.

Is this workbook enough or do I also need the book *Every Man's Battle*?

Included in the studies you'll find a few featured excerpts from the book *Every Man's Battle,* each one marked at the beginning and end by this symbol: 📖. But you really do need to read along in the book *Every Man's Battle* to truly get the most out of this companion workbook. (You'll find the appropriate chapters to read listed at the beginning of each weekly study.)

The lessons look long. Do I need to work through everything in each one?

This workbook is designed to promote your thorough exploration of all the content, but you may find it best to focus your time and discussion on some sections and questions more than others.

To help your pacing, we've designed the workbook so it can most easily be used in either an eight-week or twelve-week approach.

- *For the eight-week track,* simply follow along with the basic organization already set up with the eight different weekly lessons.

- *For the twelve-week track,* the lessons labeled Weeks Two, Five, Six, and Seven can be divided into two parts (you'll see the dividing place marked in the text).

(In addition, of course, you may decide to follow at a different pace— faster or slower—whether you're going through the workbook individually or as part of a group.)

Above all, keep in mind that the purpose of this workbook is to help guide you in specific life-application of the biblical truths taught in *Every Man's Battle.* The wide questions included in each weekly study are meant to help you approach this practical application from different angles and with personal reflection and self-examination. Allowing adequate time to prayerfully reflect on each question will be much more valuable for you than rushing through the workbook.

How do I bring together a small group to go through this workbook?
You'll get far more out of this workbook if you're able to go through it together with a small group of like-minded men. And what do you do if you don't know of any group that's going through this workbook? Start such a group of your own!

If you take a copy of the book *Every Man's Battle,* plus a copy of this companion workbook, and show them to the Christian men you know, you'll be surprised at how many will indicate interest in joining you for exploring this topic together. And it doesn't require a long commitment from them. The workbook is clearly set up so you complete one lesson per week and finish in only eight weeks—or, if you'd like to proceed at a little slower pace, you can follow the instructions provided for covering the exact same content in a twelve-week track.

Your once-per-week meeting could happen during the lunch hour one day at work, in the early morning before work begins, on a weekday evening, or even a Saturday morning. The location could be an office or meeting room at work, a room at a club or restaurant, a classroom at church, or someone's basement or den at home. Choose a location where your discussion won't be overhead by others, so the men are comfortable in sharing candidly and freely.

This workbook follows a simple design that's easy to use. First, each man in the group completes a week's lesson on his own. Then, when you come together that week, you discuss together the group questions provided under the Every Man's TALK heading in each week's lesson. Of course, if you have time, you can also discuss at length any of the other questions or topics in that week's lesson; we guarantee the men in your group will find these to be worth exploring. And they're likely as well to have plenty of their own related questions to bring up for discussion.

It's best if one person in your group is designated as the group's facilitator. This person is *not* a lecturer or teacher, but simply has the responsibility to keep the discussion moving and to ensure that each man in the group has an opportunity to fully join in.

At the beginning, remind the men of the simple ground rule that anything shared in the group *stays* in the group—everything's confidential. This will help the men feel safer about sharing honestly and openly in an environment of trust.

Finally we encourage you during each meeting together to allow time for prayer—conversational, short-sentence prayers expressed in honesty before God. Many men don't feel comfortable praying aloud before others, so in an understanding way, do all you can to help them overcome that barrier.

You're in a tough position.
You live in a world awash with sensual images available
twenty-four hours a day in a variety of mediums:
print, television, videos, the Internet—even phones.
But God offers you freedom from the slavery of sin
through the cross of Christ, and He created your eyes and mind
with an ability to be trained and controlled.
We simply have to stand up and walk by His power
in the right path. Men need a battle plan
a detailed plan for becoming a man of sexual integrity.

—from Steve Arterburn
in the introduction to *Every Man's Battle*

We need real men around here—men of honor and decency,
men with their hands where they belong
and their eyes and minds focused on Christ.
If roving eyes or sexually impure thoughts
or even sexual addictions are issues in your life,
Steve and I are hoping you'll do something about it.
Isn't it time?

—from Fred Stoeker
in the introduction to *Every Man's Battle*

where are we?

This week's reading assignment:

the introduction and chapters 1–3 in *Every Man's Battle*

Before men experience victory over sexual sin, they're hurting and confused. Why can't I win at this? they think. As the fight wears on and the losses pile higher, we begin to doubt everything about ourselves, even our salvation. At best, we think that we're deeply flawed. At worst, evil persons. We feel very alone, since men speak little of these things.

But we're not alone. Many men have fallen into their own sexual pits.

—from chapter 3 in *Every Man's Battle*

EVERY MAN'S TRUTH
(Your Personal Journey into God's Word)

As you begin this study, ask for the Holy Spirit's help in hearing and obeying His personal words for you. Read and meditate upon the following Bible passages, which have to do with God's holiness and His call to purity. Let the Lord remind you that He is calling you to purity because He has your best interest at heart. Also remember that He delights in you—as one who is made in His image and growing into His likeness, day by day.

You have heard that it was said, "Do not commit adultery."
But I tell you that anyone who looks at a woman lustfully
has already committed adultery with her in his heart.
(Matthew 5:27-28)

Who will bring any charge against those whom God has
chosen? It is God who justifies. Who is he that condemns?
Christ Jesus, who died—more than that, who was raised to
life—is at the right hand of God and is also interceding for
us. Who shall separate us from the love of Christ? Shall
trouble or hardship or persecution or famine or nakedness
or danger or sword?… No, in all these things we are more
than conquerors through him who loved us. For I am
convinced that neither death nor life, neither angels nor
demons, neither the present nor the future, nor any powers,
neither height nor depth, nor anything else in all creation,
will be able to separate us from the love of God that is in
Christ Jesus our Lord. (Romans 8:33-35,37-39)

"Come now, let us reason together,"
    says the LORD.
"Though your sins are like scarlet,
    they shall be as white as snow;
though they are red as crimson,
    they shall be like wool." (Isaiah 1:18)

1. What do Jesus' words tell you about His deep concern for your thought life?

2. What comfort do you take in Paul's words to the Roman believers? How does this passage relate to your feelings of guilt when you've given in to lust?

3. When it comes to a believer's sin, how would you distinguish between rebellion and immaturity? What is God's attitude toward us as we grow—and as we stumble—in our attempts to walk in holiness with Him? (Think about your relationship to your own children, if you have them.)

4. "White as snow" is the prophet's imagery for God's holiness. To what extent do you long for holiness and purity in your life? How are Isaiah's words hopeful to you?

☑ EVERY MAN'S CHOICE

(Questions for Personal Reflection and Examination)

📖 Pursuing sexual integrity is a controversial topic. We've been ridiculed by the world's sophisticates who find God's standard ridiculous and confining. That's fine with us, because we have a bigger concern—you. You're in a tough position. You live in a world awash with sensual images available twenty-four hours a day in a variety of mediums: print, television, videos, the Internet—even phones. 📖

📖 After teaching on the topic of male sexual purity in Sunday school, I was approached one day by a man who said, "I always thought that since I was a man I would not be able to control my roving eyes. I didn't know it could be any other way." 📖

5. Why do you think pursuing sexual integrity is such a controversial topic? How realistic is this pursuit for you?

6. How aware are you of the sensual images all around you? What has been your way of dealing with—or *not* dealing with—this bombardment of sexuality on a daily basis?

7. Have you ever considered your roving eye to be uncontrollable? In the past, when have you been most likely to lose control? What has helped you to exercise control?

 EVERY MAN'S WALK
(Your Guide to Personal Application)

📖 Steve: I can't tell you what her face looked like; nothing above the neckline registered with me that morning. My eyes feasted on this banquet of glistening flesh as she passed on my left, and they continued to follow her lithe figure as she continued jogging southbound. I turned my head further and further, craning my neck to capture every possible moment for my mental video camera.

Then *blam!* I might still be marveling at this remarkable specimen of female athleticism if my Mercedes hadn't plowed into a Chevelle that had come to a complete stop in my lane. 📖

📖 Fred: There was a monster lurking about, and it surfaced each Sunday morning when I settled in my comfy La-Z-Boy and opened the Sunday morning newspaper. I would quickly find the department-store inserts and begin paging through the colored newsprint filled with models posing in bras and panties. Always smiling. Always available. I loved lingering over each ad insert. It's wrong, I admitted, but it's such a small thing. It was a far cry from *Playboy*, I told myself. I peered through the panties, fantasizing. 📖

8. Which situations in the stories of Steve and Fred can you personally identify with most? How common do you think these situations are among the Christian men you know?

9. Think about Steve's car wreck for a moment. How much trouble have your own eyes gotten you into over the years? What especially painful incident stands out to you at the moment?

10. Fred's eyes were particularly vulnerable to the sensual newspaper ads. In what situations are your own eyes the most vulnerable? What steps have you taken so far to avoid such situations?

11. Recall that, in chapter 3, Fred speaks of the price he was paying for his sin in his relationship with God, with his wife, with his children, and with his church. In which of these areas of life do you think a man's sexual sin hurts him most quickly and obviously? How is it with you?

12. In quietness, review what you have written and learned in this week's study. If further thoughts or prayer requests come to your mind and heart, you may want to write them here.

13. a) What for you was the most meaningful concept or truth in this week's study?

b) How would you talk this over with God? Write your response here as a prayer to Him.

c) What do you believe God wants you to do in response to this
week's study?

☺☺ EVERY MAN'S TALK

(Constructive Topics and Questions for Group Discussion)

Key Highlights from the Book for Reading Aloud and Discussing

📖 Addictive sex is devoid of intimacy. Sex addicts are utterly
self-focused. They cannot achieve genuine intimacy because
their self-obsession leaves no room for giving to others.…
Addictive sex is used to escape pain and problems. The
escapist nature of addictive sex is often one of the clearest
indicators that it is present. 📖

📖 When we're fractionally addicted, we surely experience
addictive drawings, but we aren't compelled to act to salve
some pain. We're compelled by the chemical high and
the sexual gratification it brings. Another way of looking at
the scope of the problem is to picture a bell curve. According
to our experiences, we figure around 10 percent of men
have no sexual-temptation problem with their eyes and
their minds. At the other end of the curve, we figure there's
another 10 percent of men who are sexual addicts and have
a serious problem with lust.… The rest of us comprise the

middle 80 percent, living in various shades of gray when it comes to sexual sin. 📖

📖 [From The Heart of a Woman] "When my husband and I talked about this, he was honest," Deena conveyed, "and I was very angry with him. I was hurt. I felt deeply betrayed because I'd been dieting and working out to keep my weight down so that I would always look nice to him. I couldn't figure out why he still needed to look at other women."

Women told us that they struggle between pity and anger, and their feelings may ebb and flow with the tide of their husband's battle. Let us direct this advice to women reading this book: Though you know you should pray for him and fulfill him sexually, sometimes you won't want to. Talk to each other openly and honestly, then do the right thing. 📖

Discussion Questions

A. Which parts of chapters 1-3 in *Every Man's Battle* were most helpful or encouraging to you and why?

B. How would you summarize the difference between normal sexual desire and addictive sex?

C. Do you agree that sex can be a way of trying to escape inner pain? What is your own experience with this?

D. How would you explain to another man what the authors define as fractional addiction?

E. To what extent do you agree or disagree with the book's contention that, for most men, our sexual sin is based on pleasure-highs rather than true addiction?

F. Look together at The Heart of a Woman quotation. What is most surprising to you in the comments of this woman? What is most helpful to you in better understanding your own wife?

G. Do you agree with the authors' advice to wives? Talk about it together.

H. As an additional group-discussion option, look together at the text under the heading The Heart of a Woman at the end of this week's reading. What is most surprising to you in the comments of these women? What is most helpful to you in better understanding your own wife?

how we got here (part A)

This week's reading assignment:

chapters 4–5 in *Every Man's Battle*

For most of us, becoming ensnared by sexual sin happened easily and naturally, like slipping off an icy log.... Perhaps you've mustered the hope that you would someday be free from sexual sin and expected to grow out of it as naturally as you grew into it—like outgrowing acne. Perhaps you waited with each birthday for your sexual impurity to clear up. It never did. Later you assumed you'd be freed naturally through marriage. But—as for many of us—that didn't happen either.

—from chapter 4 in *Every Man's Battle*

📖 EVERY MAN'S TRUTH
(Your Personal Journey into God's Word)

Read and meditate upon the following Bible passages, which deal with God's judgment and mercy—a combination powerfully demonstrated at the Cross of Christ. There, God's *judgment* upon sin *mercifully* freed us from having to experience its destruction. As you study, remember that God's plan is to set sinners free and then use them to teach others.

Be imitators of God, therefore, as dearly loved children
and live a life of love, just as Christ loved us and gave
himself up for us as a fragrant offering and sacrifice
to God.

But among you there must not be even a hint of sexual
immorality, or of any kind of impurity.…

For you were once darkness, but now you are light in the
Lord. Live as children of light (for the fruit of the light con-
sists in all goodness, righteousness and truth) and find out
what pleases the Lord. (Ephesians 5:1-3,8-10)

It is God's will that you should be sanctified: that you
should avoid sexual immorality; that each of you should
learn to control his own body in a way that is holy and honorable, not in passionate lust like the heathen, who do not
know God; and that in this matter no one should wrong his
brother or take advantage of him. The Lord will punish men
for all such sins, as we have already told you and warned
you. For God did not call us to be impure, but to live a
holy life. (1 Thessalonians 4:3-7)

Have mercy on me, O God,
    according to your unfailing love;
according to your great compassion
    blot out my transgressions.…
Restore to me the joy of your salvation
    and grant me a willing spirit, to sustain me.
Then I will teach transgressors your ways,
    and sinners will turn back to you.
        (Psalm 51:1,12-13)

1. What does Christ's self-sacrifice mean to you? How is it a compelling motive for holy living?

2. What does it mean for you, personally, to live as a child of the light? How can you tell when you're becoming vulnerable to the darkness?

3. How do you respond to the prospect of punishment for sin? In the past, what has been the best motivator, or encourager, to keep you from sexual impurity? What have you been doing to strengthen this motivation in your life?

4. First offer the words of Psalm 51 to God as a heartfelt prayer of your own. Then take a moment to envision how God might use you in the future to minister to another man regarding sexual purity.

☑ EVERY MAN'S CHOICE

(Questions for Personal Reflection and Examination)

📖 When Mark signed up for my premarriage class, he told me, "The whole problem of impurity has been a mess. I've been hooked for years, and I'm counting on marriage to free me. I'll be able to have sex whenever I want it. Satan won't be able to tempt me at all!"

When we got together a few years later, I wasn't surprised to hear that marriage hadn't fixed the problem. Mark said, "You know, Fred…I don't want to seem like a sex addict or anything, but I probably have as many unmet desires now as I did before marriage." 📖

📖 Freedom from sexual sin rarely comes through marriage or the passage of time. (The phrase "dirty old man" should tell us something about that.) So if you're tired of sexual impurity and of the mediocre, distant relationship with God that results from it, quit waiting for marriage or some hormone drop to save the day. If you want to change, recognize that you're impure because you've diluted God's standard of sexual purity with your own. 📖

5. If you were Fred in the conversation above, how would you respond to Mark?

6. Do you agree that marriage isn't necessarily the "cure" for sexual impurity? What are the practical implications of this for you?

7. If you've been involved in sexual impurity, how have you experienced the distant relationship with God referred to by the authors?

8. What kinds of diluting attitudes or actions have you exhibited over the years?

Every Man's WALK
(Your Guide to Personal Application)

> Sometimes we're simply naive. On his way to school, Pinocchio met some scoundrels who painted a wonderful picture of spending the day at a place called Adventure Island, a sort of amusement park just offshore. He didn't know that at day's end all the boys would be turned into donkeys and be sold to pull carts in the coal mines....

But sometimes we choose wrong sexual standards not because we're naive, but simply because we're rebellious. We're like Lampwick, a swaggering boy who takes the lead in diverting Pinocchio to Adventure Island.... Perhaps, with a rebelliousness like Lampwick's, you know sexual immorality is wrong, but you do it anyway. You love your trips to Adventure Island, despite the hidden price you pay at the end of the day. 📖

📖 It is holy and honorable to completely avoid sexual immorality—to repent of it, to flee from it, and to put it to death in our lives, as we live by the Spirit. We've spent enough time living like pagans in passionate lust. 📖

9. When it comes to succumbing to temptation, would you say you are (a) mostly naive, like Pinocchio, or (b) mostly rebellious, like Lampwick?

10. What kinds of hidden prices have you paid at the end of a day on Adventure Island? (Take a moment to sit quietly with your regret and sadness over this. Invite the Lord's presence as you experience this pain.)

11. Prayerfully consider: What will it take for me to completely avoid sexual immorality in the weeks and years ahead? (Think about any changes in your self-image and/or God-image that may be required. Also consider what forms of accountability you may need to establish.)

12. In quietness, review what you have written and learned in this week's study. If further thoughts or prayer requests come to your mind and heart, you may want to write them here.

👨👩 EVERY MAN'S TALK

(Constructive Topics and Questions for Group Discussion)

Key Highlights from the Book for Reading Aloud and Discussing

📖 Sex has different meanings to men and women. Men primarily receive intimacy just before and during intercourse. Women gain intimacy through touching, sharing, hugging, and communication. Is it any wonder that the frequency of sex is less important to women than to men? 📖

📖 Larry found Linda to be far more interested in her career than in fulfilling him sexually. Not only was she disinterested in sex, she often used it as a manipulative weapon to get her own way. Consequently, Larry doesn't have sex very often. Twice a month is a bonanza, and once every two months is the norm. What's Larry supposed to say to God? 📖

📖 We aren't victims of some vast conspiracy to ensnare us sexually; we've simply chosen to mix in our own standards of sexual conduct with God's standard. Since we found God's standard too difficult, we created a mixture—something new, something comfortable, something mediocre. 📖

Discussion Questions

A. Which parts of chapter 4 in *Every Man's Battle* were most helpful or encouraging to you and why?

B. Do you agree with the authors' description of how sex has different meanings to men and women? (Optional: How would you add to or modify this statement to make it more relevant to your situation?)

C. Answer the question that comes at the end of Larry's story: What is he supposed to say to God? If you were Larry's best friend, how would you counsel him?

D. If a man has mixed his sexuality standards with God's, what first steps can he take to get back on track? (Brainstorm together about practical actions a man can take, based upon your experience and/or study so far.)

E. In your own words, and in a practical way that would be helpful for Christian men today, how would you summarize God's standards for sexual purity?

Note: If you're following a twelve-week track, save the rest of this lesson for the following week. If you're on the eight-week track...then keep going.

☑ EVERY MAN'S CHOICE
(Questions for Personal Reflection and Examination)

📖 Is it profitable for Christians to stop short at the middle ground of excellence where costs are low, balanced somewhere between paganism and obedience? Not at all! While in business it's profitable to seem perfect, in the spiritual realm it's merely comfortable to seem perfect.... Excellence is a mixed standard, while obedience is a fixed standard. We want to shoot for the fixed standard. 📖

📖 If we don't kill every hint of immorality, we'll be captured by our tendency as males to draw sexual gratification and chemical highs through our eyes. But we can't deal with our maleness until we first reject our right to mix standards. As we ask "How holy can I be?" we must pray and commit to a new relationship with God, fully aligned with His call to obedience. 📖

13. How *would* you explain the difference between (a) the pursuit of excellence and (b) the pursuit of perfection (through obedience)?

14. Do you believe you have a right to at least sometimes mix your own standards with God's?

15. Consider the difference in attitude reflected in these two personal questions: (a) How far can I go and still be called a Christian? (b) How holy can I be? How would these attitudes likely manifest themselves in a man's actions?

👟 EVERY MAN'S WALK
(Your Guide to Personal Application)

> 📖 God is your Father and expects obedience. Having given you the Holy Spirit as your power source, He believes His command should be enough for you, just as you believe

your command should be enough for your kids. Trouble is, we aren't in search of obedience. We're in search of mere excellence, and His command is not enough. We push back, responding, "Why should I eliminate every hint? That's too hard!" 📖

📖 What's your Christian life costing you? It costs something to *learn* about Christ. It costs a lot to *live* like Christ. It costs something to join a few thousand men at a conference to sing praises to God and learn how we should live; it costs a lot to come home and remain committed to the changes you said you'd make in your life.... It costs a lot to control your eyes and mind daily. 📖

16. How would you respond to someone who says: "Why should I eliminate every hint of sexual impurity?"

17. Think through some of the impure temptations and/or practices you've been able to eliminate from your days so far. What hints still remain?

18. Realistically, what is it costing you these days to be a Christian? Try making a list of some of your spiritual price tags. What insight does this list offer?

19. What will likely be the next challenge for you, just over the horizon, when it comes to controlling your eyes and mind? What preparations have you made in order to be ready for the onslaught of temptation?

20. a) What for you was the most meaningful concept or truth in this week's study?

b) How would you talk this over with God? Write your response here as a prayer to Him.

c) What do you believe God wants you to do in response to this week's study?

👨👩 EVERY MAN'S TALK
(More Topics and Questions for Group Discussion)

Key Highlights from the Book for Reading Aloud and Discussing

📖 Let me demonstrate the difference between excellence and obedience: During transitions between sizes, Brenda often hoped to wear something from her smaller-sized wardrobe to church. Squeezing into it, she'd ask me, "Is this too tight?" Often it was a close call, and I would have to choose between modifying the truth or hurting her feelings and discouraging her. Was it okay for me to modify the truth to avoid this unpleasantness? What would you do? Would you modify the truth? 📖

📖 I organized an intercessors' group during our church's Wednesday night services, simply opening a room for ninety minutes of intercession for our congregation. The first night, a half-dozen people came to the door and asked, "Is this the room where they're teaching about intercession?"

"No, we won't be teaching about intercession," I answered. "We're going to be interceding." Each person turned away to leave. It feels good to learn about intercession, but it's a costly thing to do. The same can be said about purity. 📖

📖 Sexual impurity has become rampant in the church because we've ignored the costly work of obedience to God's standards as individuals, asking too often, "How far can I go and still be called a Christian?" We've crafted an image and may even seem sexually pure while permitting our eyes to play freely when no one is around, avoiding the hard work of being sexually pure. 📖

Discussion Questions

F. Which parts of chapter 5 in *Every Man's Battle* were most helpful or encouraging to you and why?

G. How do you typically answer the question: "Is this dress too tight"? Once the laughter dies down, spend some time in serious discussion about men's tendencies to modify the truth in their approach to sexual purity.

H. Why is it so much easier to learn about prayer than to pray? to learn about purity than to practice purity? What are some of the highest costs involved?

I. Look together at the story of King Josiah in 2 Chronicles 34. Read aloud verse 8 and verses 14-33. How do you see Josiah's example in this passage as a model of obedience? What else is Josiah's example here a model of?

J. When are your eyes most likely to play freely? Talk together about actions or attitudes that help you control your eyes. (Be willing to share what works for you.)

how we got here (part B)

This week's reading assignment:

chapters 6–7 in *Every Man's Battle*

You stand before an important battle. You've decided that the slavery of sexual sin isn't worth your love of sexual sin. You're committed to removing every hint of it. But how? Your maleness looms as your own worse enemy.

You got into this mess by being male; you'll get out by being a man.

—from chapter 7 in *Every Man's Battle*

📖 EVERY MAN'S TRUTH
(Your Personal Journey into God's Word)

As you begin this study, ask for the Holy Spirit's help in hearing and obeying His personal words for you. Read and meditate upon the following Bible passages, which have to do with God's call to faithfulness in marriage. As you read, realize that God is not calling you to anything that's foreign to Himself. The Scriptures proclaim, over and over again, the Lord's utter faithfulness...to *you!*

You shall not commit adultery. (Exodus 20:14)

For these commands are a lamp,
this teaching is a light,
and the corrections of discipline
are the way to life,
keeping you from the immoral woman,
from the smooth tongue of the wayward wife.
Do not lust in your heart after her beauty
or let her captivate you with her eyes,
for the prostitute reduces you to a loaf of bread,
and the adulteress preys upon your very life.
Can a man scoop fire into his lap
without his clothes being burned?
Can a man walk on hot coals
without his feet being scorched?...
But a man who commits adultery lacks judgment;
whoever does so destroys himself.
(Proverbs 6:23-28,32)

He will cover you with his feathers,
and under his wings you will find refuge;
his faithfulness will be your shield and rampart.
(Psalm 91:4)

1. What are some of the horrible consequences of lust and adultery?
   How does a man destroy himself in the arms of another woman?

2. When you think of God's faithfulness to you, what events or circumstances of the past spring to mind? (Spend some quiet moments in thankfulness and praise.)

3. How does it feel to know that God's love is like the warm and close protection that a hen offers its young? How can God's faithfulness act as a "shield" and "rampart" in your life?

4. How easy or difficult is it for you, after you have fallen to temptation, to immediately move back under God's "wing"? Why?

☑ EVERY MAN'S CHOICE
(Questions for Personal Reflection and Examination)

📖 For males, impurity of the eyes is sexual foreplay. That's right. Just like stroking an inner thigh or rubbing a breast. Because foreplay is any sexual action that naturally takes us down the road to intercourse. Foreplay ignites passions, rocketing us by stages until we go all the way.... No doubt about it: Visual sexual gratification is a form of sex for men. As males, we draw sexual gratification and chemical highs through our eyes. 📖

📖 In a newsletter, author and speaker Dr. Gary Rosberg told of seeing a pair of hands that reminded him of the hands of his father, who had gone on to heaven. Gary continued to reminisce about what his father's hands meant to him. Then he shifted his thoughts to the hands of Jesus, noting this simple truth: "They were hands that never touched a woman with dishonor." 📖

5. Have you ever before considered the dangers of visual foreplay? What is your reaction to the authors' statements about it?

6. What role is visual sexual gratification playing in your life these days? What is your level of awareness of it?

7. Think about the reputation of Jesus' hands for a moment. Then consider: What legacy will your hands leave behind?

8. Read Galatians 6:7-8. How have you seen the truth of this principle in your own life?

EVERY MAN'S WALK
(Your Guide to Personal Application)

I (Fred) remember the moment when it all broke loose. I'd failed God with my eyes for the thirty-millionth time. My heart churned in guilt, pain, and sorrow. Driving down Merle Hay Road, I suddenly gripped the wheel and through clenched teeth, I yelled out: "That's it! I'm through with this! I'm making a covenant with my eyes. I don't care what it takes, and I don't care if I die trying. It stops here. It stops here!"

I made that covenant and built it brick by brick. My breakthrough:

- I made a clear decision.
- I decided once and for all to make a change.

I wasn't fully convinced I could trust myself even then, but I'd finally and truly engaged the battle. Through my covenant with my eyes, all my mental and spiritual resources were now leveled upon a single target: my impurity. With that covenant I had also chosen manhood, to rise above my natural male tendencies. That was a huge step for me. 📖

📖 Was God proud of Job? You bet! In Job 31:1, we see Job making this startling revelation: "I made a covenant with my eyes not to look lustfully at a girl."

A covenant with his eyes! You mean he made a promise with his eyes to not gaze upon a young woman? It's not possible! It can't be true!

Yet Job was successful; otherwise, he wouldn't have made this promise: "If my heart has been enticed by a woman, or if I have lurked at my neighbor's door, then may my wife grind another man's grain, and may other men sleep with her" (31:9-10). 📖

9. Fred had failed "thirty million" times. How many times has it been for you? Do you believe it will take a crisis-point event like Fred's to bring you to a place of choosing covenant making? Why or why not?

10. Have you ever sensed that the grace of God was the only way out of your cycle of failed will power? How did you respond?

11. What does it mean for you to rest in God's saving grace? How will you know when you are ready to make that your standard response during the toughest temptations?

12. If you were to make a covenant with your eyes right now, how would you write it? Jot your statement here:

13. In quietness, review what you have written and learned in this week's study. If further thoughts or prayer requests come to your mind and heart, you may want to write them here.

14. a) What for you was the most meaningful concept or truth in this week's study?

b) How would you talk this over with God? Write your response here as a prayer to Him.

c) What do you believe God wants you to do in response to this week's study?

👥 EVERY MAN'S TALK

(Constructive Topics and Questions for Group Discussion)

Key Highlights from the Book for Reading Aloud and Discussing

📖 Author George Gilder in *Sexual Suicide* reported that men commit more than 90 percent of major crimes of violence, 100 percent of the rapes, and 95 percent of the burglaries. Men comprise 94 percent of our drunken drivers, 70 percent of suicides, 91 percent of offenders against family and children. Most often, the chief perpetrators are single men.

Our maleness brings a natural, uniquely male form of rebelliousness. This natural tendency gives us the arrogance needed to stop short of God's standards. As men, we'll often choose sin simply because we like our own way. 📖

📖 "If I'm going to be out all week on business," Rob told us, "Sue and I usually have sex on Sunday night. She's pretty good at helping out that way, and I need the help. On Monday night when I'm on the road, I have dinner, do a little work, catch CNN, and go to bed. I may think about sex, but it's no big deal. By Wednesday night, however, I'm not the same man. I practically feel possessed! The temptations are horrible, and they seem to rise in intensity each night." 📖

📖 When it comes down to it, God's definition of real manhood is pretty simple: It means hearing His Word and doing it. That's God's only definition of manhood—a doer of the Word. And God's definition of a sissy is someone who hears the Word of God and doesn't do it. 📖

Discussion Questions

A. Which parts of chapters 6 and 7 in *Every Man's Battle* were most helpful or encouraging to you and why?

B. Males are rebellious by nature. Obviously this trait is not a gift from God but a result of our sinful nature as fallen human beings. Think about other maleness traits. To what degree is each one a gift from God, and to what degree is each one a result of our sinful nature?

C. To what extent can you relate to Rob's struggles? What is your advice for him?

D. How would you describe the difference between maleness and manhood?

E. Do you totally buy into the conclusion that a real man is one who is a doer of the Word of God? Why or why not?

F. How important is the fellowship of other Christian men when it comes to your ability to be a doer of the Word? What are the opportunities for forming accountability relationships within your group? Talk about it!

G. As an additional group-discussion option, look together at the text under the heading The Heart of a Woman at the end of this week's reading. What is most surprising to you in the comments of these women? What is most helpful to you in better understanding your own wife?

choosing victory (part A)

This week's reading assignment:

chapter 8 in *Every Man's Battle*

When you talk to courageous World War II veterans, they say they don't feel like heroes. They simply had a job to do. When the landing-craft ramps fell open, they swallowed hard and said, "It's time." Time to fight.

In your struggle with sexual impurity, isn't it time? Sure, fighting back will be hard. But your life and home are under a withering barrage of machine-gun sexuality that rakes the landscape mercilessly. Right now you're in a landing craft, inching closer to shore and a showdown. God has given you the weapons and trained you for battle.

You can't stay in the landing craft forever.

—from chapter 8 in *Every Man's Battle*

📖 Every Man's TRUTH

(Your Personal Journey into God's Word)

As you begin this study, read and meditate upon the following Bible passages, which have to do with your identity and power in Christ. Remember that Christ has already fought the battle against sin on your behalf—and won. Now it is time to live in that victory every day.

Grace and peace be yours in abundance through the knowledge of God and of Jesus our Lord.

His divine power has given us everything we need for life and godliness through our knowledge of him who called us by his own glory and goodness. Through these he has given us his very great and precious promises, so that through them you may participate in the divine nature and escape the corruption in the world caused by evil desires. (2 Peter 1:2-4)

Now if we died with Christ, we believe that we will also live with him. For we know that since Christ was raised from the dead, he cannot die again; death no longer has mastery over him. The death he died, he died to sin once for all; but the life he lives, he lives to God.

In the same way, count yourselves dead to sin but alive to God in Christ Jesus. Therefore do not let sin reign in your mortal body so that you obey its evil desires. Do not offer the parts of your body to sin, as instruments of wickedness, but rather offer yourselves to God, as those who have been brought from death to life; and offer the parts of your body to him as instruments of righteousness. For sin shall not be your master, because you are not under law, but under grace....

You have been set free from sin and have become slaves to righteousness. (Romans 6:8-14,18)

1. According to Peter, what exactly has God given you? What is the source of your ability to "participate in the divine nature"? When have you most powerfully sensed the glory and goodness of Jesus in your life?

2. If we have everything we need for godliness, what is holding us back from constant, lifelong sexual purity? (Think about what it means to count yourself dead to sin.)

3. In the heat of sexual temptation, what will it mean for you to *not* "offer…your body to sin," as Paul says? What will offering yourself to God require at that point? (Give some thought to the role your will power can play—and *can't* play—at this point in the battle.)

4. Have you ever known someone who was a slave to righteousness? What can you learn from him or her?

☑ EVERY MAN'S CHOICE

(Questions for Personal Reflection and Examination)

📖 I was angry. I wanted to win right away and to win decisively—not somewhere down the road where age might bring victory through the back door. I wanted to win when the battle was hottest.

You should too. If you don't win now, you'll never know whether you're truly a man of God. 📖

📖 We've known those who have failed in their battle for sexual purity, and we know some who have won. The difference? Those who won hated their impurity. They were going to war and were going to win—or die trying. Every resource was leveled upon the foe.

There will be no victory in this area of your life until you choose manhood with all your might. 📖

5. How angry are you about the battle? On a scale of one to ten, how convinced are you that God's will is for you to win the battle and be sexually pure?

6. On a scale of one to ten, to what extent would you say you truly hate the sin of sexual impurity in any form?

7. On a scale of one to ten, to what extent would you say you truly expect to win the battle for sexual purity? What are your reasons for picking this score?

 EVERY MAN'S **WALK**

(Your Guide to Personal Application)

📖 Listen to the words spoken by preacher Steve Hill, who was addressing escape from addiction to drugs and alcohol as well as from sexual sin: "There's no temptation that is uncommon to man. God will send you a way of escape, but you've got to be willing to take that way of escape, friend." 📖

📖 Admit it: You love your sexual highs, but slavery engulfs you. Is the love worth the loathing?

Look in the mirror. Are you proud of your sexual fantasizing? Or do you feel degraded after viewing lingerie ads or sex scenes in films?

Sexually speaking, you have a low-grade sexual fever. It doesn't disable you, but you aren't healthy either. You can sort of function normally, but you can't really push hard. Basically, you just get by. And if this fever doesn't break, you'll never fully function as a Christian. Like the prodigal son, you need to come to your senses and make a decision. 📖

8. What is your strongest motivation for achieving and maintaining sexual purity?

9. Recall some of the times when you gave in to sexual temptation. Was there always a "way of escape" open to you? In a particular instance, what do you think kept you from taking the escape route?

10. Answer Steve and Fred's question as honestly as you can: "Is the love worth the loathing"? (Suggestion: For a few minutes, turn your awareness to Christ's abiding presence. Just you and Jesus—sit quietly with your response.)

11. Read Romans 12:1-2. Imagine completely giving up sexual fantasy in your life. How much grief would that bring you? Are you ready to experience that pain as an act of sacrificial worship?

12. In quietness, review what you have written and learned in this week's study. If further thoughts or prayer requests come to your mind and heart, you may want to write them here.

13. a) What for you was the most meaningful concept or truth in this week's study?

b) How would you talk this over with God? Write your response here as a prayer to Him.

c) What do you believe God wants you to do in response to this week's study?

🙂🗣 EVERY MAN'S TALK

(Constructive Topics and Questions for Group Discussion)

Key Highlights from the Book for Reading Aloud and Discussing

📖 Kirk, a worker in a local ministry, was caught in the early stages of an affair. By talking dirty, he'd been pushing a coworker toward a compromising situation. He said he wanted my help, and I (Fred) agreed to meet with Kirk and his pastor.

In our first meeting, the pastor said, "In our community, this kind of talk and behavior is commonplace." I saw Kirk nod his head in agreement. I didn't meet with Kirk again because I knew he didn't hate his sin. 📖

📖 Sexual impurity isn't like a tumor growing out of control inside us. We treat it that way when our prayers focus on deliverance, as we plead for someone to come remove it. Actually, sexual impurity is a series of bad decisions on our part—a result of immature character—and deliverance won't deliver you into instant maturity. Character work needs to be done.

Holiness is not some nebulous thing. It's a series of right choices.... You'll be holy when you choose not to sin. You're already free from the *power* of sexual immorality; you are not yet free from the *habit* of sexual immorality, until you choose to be. 📖

📖 God knows the provision He's made for us. We aren't short on power or authority, but what we lack is urgency.

We must choose to be strong and courageous to walk into purity. In the millisecond it takes to make that choice, the Holy Spirit will start guiding you and walking through the struggle with you. 📖

Discussion Questions

A. Which parts of chapter 8 in *Every Man's Battle* were most helpful or encouraging to you and why?

B. Discuss the case of Kirk. Was Fred right in not meeting with him again? Explain.

C. Consider the out-of-control tumor analogy. Why do we tend to think of sexual impurity as a disease that attacks us? How is this a cop-out?

D. What is wrong with praying for deliverance year after year?

E. Describe, as clearly and concisely as you can, the provision God has made for us.

F. Talk in practical terms about what choosing means to you.

G. Take a few moments as a group to reflect silently on these questions as they apply and relate to you: (1) How long are you going to stay sexually impure? (2) How long will you rob your wife sexually? (3) How long will you stunt the growth of oneness with your wife, a oneness you promised her years ago?

choosing victory (part B)

This week's reading assignment:

chapters 9–10 in *Every Man's Battle*

Okay, so you've decided it's time to fight. And you realize that your battle for sexual purity will cost you something. It will require sacrifice, intensity, and honor. But let's get something else in clear view: What can you expect to gain by choosing manhood and the purity that goes with it?

By winning this war, your life will be blessed in tremendous ways. Your victory will recover what was lost through sin. Victory will help you regain and revitalize your relationship with God, your wife, your children, and your ministry.

—from chapter 9 in *Every Man's Battle*

EVERY MAN'S TRUTH
(Your Personal Journey into God's Word)

The following Bible passages continue with the theme of our identity and power in Christ. As you consider their message, ask the Holy Spirit to lead you into specific, practical applications for your daily life.

> Do you not know that your bodies are members of Christ
> himself? Shall I then take the members of Christ and unite

them with a prostitute? Never! Do you not know that he who unites himself with a prostitute is one with her in body? For it is said, "The two will become one flesh." But he who unites himself with the Lord is one with him in spirit.

Flee from sexual immorality. All other sins a man commits are outside his body, but he who sins sexually sins against his own body. (1 Corinthians 6:15-18)

We take captive every thought to make it obedient to Christ. (2 Corinthians 10:5)

I keep asking that the God of our Lord Jesus Christ, the glorious Father, may give you the Spirit of wisdom and revelation, so that you may know him better. I pray also that the eyes of your heart may be enlightened in order that you may know the hope to which he has called you, the riches of his glorious inheritance in the saints, and his incomparably great power for us who believe. That power is like the working of his mighty strength, which he exerted in Christ when he raised him from the dead and seated him at his right hand in the heavenly realms, far above all rule and authority, power and dominion, and every title that can be given, not only in the present age but also in the one to come. (Ephesians 1:17-21)

1. According to 1 Corinthians 6 above, what is a major implication of being a member of Christ? Have you ever thought of your body as being a part of Christ? What does this mean to you?

2. When are your thoughts typically most "captive"? When are they most likely to roam free?

3. Paul wanted believers to know Jesus better. How can knowing Him well help us stay sexually pure? How can knowing Him better, day by day, bring power into our lives? (Think about some practical applications to your own battle.)

☑ Every Man's CHOICE

(Questions for Personal Reflection and Examination)

> 📖 Because of sin, I (Fred) hadn't been able to look at myself in a mirror for years. While I knew God loved me unconditionally, I also knew He didn't unconditionally approve of my behavior. Consequently, I couldn't look God in the eye.
>
> Once I heard a pastor preach, "When Jesus knocks, He wants freedom to enter every room in your house. In every part of your life, He wants to be welcome and comfortable. Is He locked out of any room in your house?" 📖

📖 I (Fred) was a prodigal eating old cobs of corn left in a pigsty. To restore my relationship with my Father, I had to get up out of the mud and start walking home. I didn't have to clean myself up first, but I did have to make that first step. On the road ahead, the Father would be waiting with a ring, a robe, shoes, and everything else an honored son was meant to have. But first I had to come to my senses, as I did that day on Merle Hay Road when I took my first step toward home— toward purity—by making that covenant with my eyes. 📖

4. Can you look at yourself in the mirror these days? Can you look God in the eye? Think about it...

5. Make a list of the rooms in your inner "house" where Jesus is welcome and unwelcome. What keeps certain rooms off-limits to Him, even though He already knows what's there? (Suggestion: Spend some moments, right now, letting Jesus into the ugliest rooms. Tell Him of the longing, desire, pain, and so on, that has helped you "furnish" those rooms over the years. This is an opportunity to open your whole heart to Him.)

6. If you see some aspects of the prodigal son within you, where are you in your journey? Are you still heading for adventure in the big, wide world? suffering loss and desperation? on your way back home?

EVERY MAN'S WALK
(Your Guide to Personal Application)

📖 One of the things I (Steve) brought into my marriage with Sandy was a secret compartment I'd guarded for years. Inside it was a girlfriend from much earlier in my life, the first true love I really had. I considered this secret compartment to be mine forever, a private place out of which I could draw fond old memories. It wasn't until I was willing to give up that secret compartment that I was fully able to connect with Sandy. 📖

📖 Likewise, sin can affect families for generations, as it did in mine. I came from a family in which the men loved sex and pornography and ditched their wives or were caught up in affairs....

My sixteen-year-old son, Jasen, is now a handsome, strapping, six-foot adolescent with an easy smile and friendly ways. Not long ago Jasen was with friends who had some pornography. He walked away. My son walked away. You don't understand what that means to me! 📖

7. To what extent can you relate to Steve's secret compartment? Do you have any compartments labeled Old Girlfriends or Pornography or Favorite Web Sites? What practical steps can you take—today—to begin forsaking these private, secret compartments?

8. How have you been affected by the sins of your fathers? How do you think you are affecting your own children's lives through your secret sins of impurity?

9. Be Fred for a moment. How do you feel after discovering that Jasen walked away from pornography? Would your son (or any child who looks to your example) walk away?

10. As you think of attaining the sexual purity that is God's will for you, how do you envision your relationship with God in the near future? your relationship with your wife? your future legacy for your children? your ministry in the church, both in the near future and long-term?

11. In quietness, review what you have written and learned in this week's study. If further thoughts or prayer requests come to your mind and heart, you may want to write them here.

👥 EVERY MAN'S TALK
(Constructive Topics and Questions for Group Discussion)

Key Highlights from the Book for Reading Aloud and Discussing

📖 Along with inner peace comes an outer peace that affects your daily life.... Wally used to dread hotels. He can now check into a hotel at night, enjoy a meal at the coffee shop, go back to his room, shower, turn out the lights, and fall asleep. "I no longer fear hotel rooms in the slightest," he says. "Sensual things don't dominate my day as they once could. All those compelling desires that ruled me are gone, and yet my desire for my wife, Tina, still percolates rather nicely!" 📖

📖 Trust is important in the body of Christ. In
1 Corinthians 6:15-20, Paul says that not only does a
sexually immoral man sin against his own body, but he
also sins against the body of Christ and his friends
within the body. Our friends trust us to be pure; a failure
would crush their spirits as well as our own. We must
be trustworthy. 📖

📖 When your son questions what he should watch, what
he should do with the pornography other boys show him, or
what he should do when that cute girl gets him alone and
starts unbuttoning her blouse, will anyone be speaking
against it? It won't be his friends. Even his church buddies
will tell him to go for it. Your voice had better be loud and
crystal clear because it will probably be the only one whis-
pering, "Flee immorality, son." Your example must be the
argument opposing temptation. 📖

Discussion Questions

A. Which parts of chapter 9 in *Every Man's Battle* were most helpful or
encouraging to you and why?

B. Talk about Wally and the change that occurred in his life. In your opinion, how realistic is it to think that any man could come to this point—
of not being tempted by the X-rated cable channels in the motel room?

C. Talk together about the trust levels in your group, in light of the
middle quotation above. Discuss some ways you can maintain trust
with one another in the area of sexual purity.

D. Look at the quotation on the previous page just before Discussion Questions. Sit for a while in silence as each man does a personal example check within his heart. Then spend some time praying for one another's children and/or the young men in your church or community.

Note: If you're following a twelve-week track,
save the rest of this lesson for the following week.
If you're on the eight-week track…then keep going.

☑ EVERY MAN'S CHOICE
(Questions for Personal Reflection and Examination)

📖 Satan's greatest weapon against you is deception. He knows Jesus has already purchased your freedom. He also knows that once you see the simplicity of this battle, you'll win in short order, so he deceives and confuses. He tricks you into thinking you're a helpless victim, someone who'll need years of group therapy. 📖

📖 Your goal is sexual purity. Here's a good working definition of it—good because of its simplicity: You are sexually pure when no sexual gratification comes from anyone or anything but your wife.

Purity means stopping sexual gratification that comes to us from outside our marriage.… That means your objective in the war against lust is to build three perimeters of defense into your life: (1) with your eyes, (2) in your mind, and (3) in your heart. 📖

12. Have you ever viewed yourself as a helpless victim to sexual temptation? According to Steve and Fred, what is a more honest assessment?

13. What is your reaction to the authors' definition of sexual purity? To
what extent are you ready to put it into daily practice?

📚 EVERY MAN'S WALK
(Your Guide to Personal Application)

> 📖 The simple truth? Impurity is a habit. It lives like a
> habit. When some hot-looking babe walks in, your eyes
> have the bad habit of bouncing toward her, sliding up and
> down.... The fact that impurity is merely a habit comes as a
> surprise to many men.... If impurity were genetic or some
> victimizing spell, you'd be helpless. But since impurity is a
> habit, it can be changed. You have hope, because if it lives
> like a habit, it can die like a habit. (We believe it can be
> done in six weeks.) 📖

> 📖 Don't misunderstand. We're not saying your habits have
> no relationship to your emotions or circumstances. Glen told
> us, "My sexual sin became much worse when I was under a

deadline at work, and especially when my wife and I fought or I felt unloved and unappreciated. It seemed at those times that I was compelled to sin sexually and couldn't say no."

For Glen, job-related stress and lack of acceptance were *not* the root cause of his sexual impurity, however. The sexual impurity was simply one way he dealt with these emotions and circumstances. In short, he ran to impurity as an escape. But when he removed the sexual impurity, he began processing these things in other ways. 📖

14. Consider why the authors believe impurity and masturbation are habits. To what extent do you agree or disagree with their reasoning?

15. Think of some habits that you've "killed" in the past. Do you believe the impurity habit can die as well? What gives you hope?

16. Glen experienced an increased compulsion during times of stress, anger, or rejection. Can you relate? What could help you prepare for these times of particular vulnerability in the future?

17. a) What for you was the most meaningful concept or truth in this week's study?

b) How would you talk this over with God? Write your response here as a prayer to Him.

c) What do you believe God wants you to do in response to this week's study?

Every Man's TALK
(More Topics and Questions for Group Discussion)

Key Highlights from the Book for Reading Aloud and Discussing

> Because of rejection and lost love, men begin to seek for this lost love in all the wrong places. In their search, where's the path of least resistance? A pretend lover, a pornographic lover with a permanent smile. A lover who

never says no, one who never rejects. One who never abandons and is always discreet. One who supports the man's ego in the midst of his self-doubt.... This path is a *chosen* path, a path made available by the impure eyes stoking the sexual fever, providing an unending pool of lovers from which to draw. 📖

📖 While there may not be spiritual oppression involved in your battle, there'll always be spiritual opposition. The enemy is constantly near your ear. He doesn't want you to win this fight, and he knows the lies that so often break men's confidence and their will to win. Expect to hear lies and plenty of them. 📖

📖 The first issue is accountability. For many men who are willing to fight for sexual purity, an important step is finding accountability support in a men's Bible study group, in a smaller group of one or two other men serving as accountability partners, or by going into counseling.

For an accountability partner, enlist a male friend, perhaps someone older and well respected in the church, to encourage you in the heat of battle. The men's ministry at your church can also help you find someone who can pray for you and ask you the tough questions. 📖

Discussion Questions

E. Which parts of chapter 10 in *Every Man's Battle* were most helpful or encouraging to you and why?

F. What is the authors' working definition of sexual purity in this chapter? What are the three defense perimeters they say we must build to attain the goal of sexual purity?

G. The authors say: "Expect to hear lies and plenty of them." Look at Satan's arguments listed under the heading Purity Always Brings Spiritual Opposition. Which of these arguments do you think are the most powerful and dangerous? Which of the truth-responses are most encouraging to you?

H. What is your experience with seeking love in the wrong places? Do you agree this has been a choice? How does rejection or lost love tend to fuel this choice?

I. Have someone read aloud the third quote above, dealing with accountability. Then go back to the conversation in the book between Ron and Nathan. As appropriate, talk together about how these kinds of relationships could work among some of the men in your group. Do any of the men want to set up an accountability relationship at this time?

J. As an additional group-discussion option, look together at the text under the heading The Heart of a Woman at the end of this week's reading. What is most surprising to you in the comments of these women? What is most helpful to you in better understanding your own wife?

victory with your eyes

This week's reading assignment:

chapters 11-13 in *Every Man's Battle*

Why must "bouncing the eyes" be immediate? After all, you might argue, a glance isn't the same as lusting. If we define "lusting" as staring open-mouthed until drool pools at your feet, then a glance isn't the same as lusting. But if we define lusting as any look that creates that little chemical high, that little pop, then we have something a bit more difficult to measure. This chemical high happens more quickly than you realize. In our experience, drawing the line at "immediate" is clean and easy for the mind and eyes to understand.

—adapted from chapter 11 in *Every Man's Battle*

EVERY MAN'S TRUTH
(Your Personal Journey into God's Word)

Read and meditate upon the following Bible passages, which have to do with the marvelous visual aspects of God's creation. Let the Lord bless you as you remember: He gave you sight that you might enjoy all the beauty and wonder of this world. The ultimate goal, of course, is that your heart may be lifted up in praise of His awesome power and glory. Why let your eyes pursue less worthy goals?

O Lord, our Lord,

> how majestic is your name in all the earth!

You have set your glory

> above the heavens....

When I consider your heavens,

> the work of your fingers,

the moon and the stars,

> which you have set in place,

what is man that you are mindful of him,

> the son of man that you care for him?
>
> > (Psalm 8:1,3-4)

The heavens declare the glory of God;

> the skies proclaim the work of his hands.

Day after day they pour forth speech;

> night after night they display knowledge.

There is no speech or language

> where their voice is not heard.
>
> > (Psalm 19:1-3)

My eyes are ever on the Lord,

> for only he will release my feet from the snare.
>
> > (Psalm 25:15)

1. Consider the majesty of God conveyed by the heavens. When have you experienced this awesomeness in a night sky? Give thanks!

2. How can creation "display knowledge"? What have you seen of God in nature?

3. If you've been using your eyes more for lust than for worship, what would you like to say to the Lord about that right now? Consider: What practical actions might help you to keep your eyes "ever on the Lord" this day?

☑ EVERY MAN'S CHOICE
(Questions for Personal Reflection and Examination)

📖 A red-blooded American male can't watch a major sporting event without being assaulted by commercials showing a bunch of half-naked women cavorting on some beach with some beer-soaked yahoos. What's a man to do? 📖

📖 To attain sexual purity as we defined it, we must starve our eyes of the bowls of sexual gratification that come from outside our marriage. When you starve your eyes and eliminate "junk sex" from your life, you'll deeply crave "real

food"—your wife. And no wonder. She's the only thing in
the cupboard, and you're hungry! 📖

4. Think about the red-blooded American male's dilemma in front of
   the television. What is Fred's solution? Define "bouncing the eyes."

5. How many bowls of gratification do you think you receive from "junk
   sex" in a typical day? What will starving the eyes look like for you?
   And are you ready to crave your wife more deeply?

👟 EVERY MAN'S WALK
(Your Guide to Personal Application)

> 📖 I (Fred) can't define the best defense for your weaknesses,
> but let me share mine so you'll get a feel for the process.
>
> Rule 1: When my hand reached for a magazine or insert,
> if I sensed in even the slightest way that my underlying
> motive was to see something sensual, I forfeited my right to
> pick up that magazine or insert. Forever.
>
> To be honest, this didn't work well at first. 📖

> 📖 My body began to fight back in some interesting ways....
> Whenever I was taken in by one of these tricks, I'd bark to

myself in sharp rebuke, "You've made a covenant with your
eyes! You can't do that anymore." In the first two weeks, I
must have said it a million times, but the repeated confession
of truth eventually worked a transformation in me. 📖

6. Look over Fred's list of My Greatest Enemies in chapter 11. What
   would be on your own list of "obvious and prolific sources of sensual
   images apart from your wife"? (Spend plenty of time coming up with
   an accurate list that doesn't overlook any important areas.)

7. Now spend plenty of time coming up with defense tactics in each
   identified area.

8. Fred says he can't define the actual defense methods that will work
   best for you. But what did you think of his own rules? What about
   rule number one? What rules are you considering for yourself?

9. Are you ready for your body and mind to fight back, as Fred's did? What forms of inner rebellion will you likely need to prepare yourself for in this battle?

10. In quietness, review what you have written and learned in this week's study. If further thoughts or prayer requests come to your mind and heart, you may want to write them here.

EVERY MAN'S TALK

(Constructive Topics and Questions for Group Discussion)

Key Highlights from the Book for Reading Aloud and Discussing

Imagine that your current level of sexual hunger requires ten bowls of sexual gratification per week. These bowls of gratification should be filled from your single legitimate vessel, the wife whom God provided for you. But because males soak up sexual gratification through the eyes, we can effortlessly fill our bowls from other sources.

Once you're winning the battle, you'll be saying things you haven't uttered for years like, "I can't wait for tonight, baby." All your imaginative creativity now blossoms upon your marriage bed, not in some fantasy world. You'll be fully enamored with her!… She'll probably ask you what's going on, and once she learns what's cooking, you'll both need to find a new sexual equilibrium. 📖

📖 "Wait a minute, Fred," you say. "Cutting down from ten bowls to eight bowls seems unfair. I'm being cheated, all because I'm obeying God!"

I guarantee you won't feel cheated. With your whole sexual being now focused upon your wife, sex with her will be so transformed that your satisfaction will explode off any known scale. Yes, even while consuming fewer bowls. It's a personal guarantee.… You can count on a sexual payoff from obedience. 📖

Discussion Questions

A. Which parts of chapters 11 and 12 in *Every Man's Battle* were most helpful or encouraging to you and why?

B. What is your reaction to the bowls analogy? How helpful is it for you to view your sexual need this way? Why?

C. How do you think most wives will respond to a husband who's newly enamored with her? How would you counsel a friend in this situation, as he helps his wife learn what's going on?

D. In your opinion, what percentage of men will likely react to starving the eyes with: "I'm being cheated"? Why? What is the authors' response?

Note: If you're following a twelve-week track,
save the rest of this lesson for the following week.
If you're on the eight-week track…then keep going.

☑ EVERY MAN'S CHOICE
(Questions for Personal Reflection and Examination)

📖 You'll need a good Bible verse to use as a sword and rallying point…. But your shield—a protective verse that you can reflect on and draw strength from even when you aren't in the direct heat of battle—may be even more important than your sword, because it places temptation out of earshot. 📖

11. Why do you need a "sword" and "shield," according to this chapter? What is their value in your pursuit of sexual purity?

12. What are the merits of Job 31:1 as a "sword" verse? As a challenge to this verse, what thoughts or arguments do you think Satan and his forces would be likely to use?

13. What are the merits of 1 Corinthians 6:18-20 as a "shield" passage? As a challenge to this passage, what thoughts or arguments do you think Satan and his forces would be likely to use?

14. What aspects of the authors' strategy for bouncing and starving the eyes make the most sense to you? What questions do you still have about these plans?

🥾 EVERY MAN'S WALK
(Your Guide to Personal Application)

📖 Suddenly an old girlfriend pops into your mind. Note the great difference in perspective between the following two possible responses:

1. Should I daydream about my old girlfriend right now?
2. I don't even have the right to ask such a question, because I don't have the authority to make that decision.

The first response implies that you have the authority and the right to make that decision. The second implies that the question itself is moot. 📖

📖 In the long term, do you still have to monitor your eyes? Yes, because the natural bent of your eyes is to sin, and you'll return to bad habits if you're careless. But with only the slightest effort, good habits are permanent....

After a year or so—though it may take longer—nearly all major skirmishes will stop. Bouncing your eyes will become deeply entrenched. Your brain, now policing itself tightly, will rarely slip anymore, having given up long ago on its chances to return to the old days of pornographic pleasure-highs. 📖

15. What verses will you select for your "sword" and for your "shield"?

16. What are some of the important questions in the realm of sexual temptation that you no longer have a right to ask yourself?

17. What kind of short-term results and reactions do you expect in your pursuit of sexual purity? What kind of long-term results and reactions do you expect in your pursuit of sexual purity?

18. In your own life, what do you believe are the most important factors that will ensure the success of this entire strategy for purity through your eyes?

19. a) What for you was the most meaningful concept or truth in this week's study?

b) How would you talk this over with God? Write your response here as a prayer to Him.

c) What do you believe God wants you to do in response to this week's study?

👤👤 EVERY MAN'S TALK

(More Topics and Questions for Group Discussion)

Key Highlights from the Book for Reading Aloud and Discussing

📖 Once on an overnight hotel stay, I walked down the hall-way to the ice machine. On top of the machine was a *Playboy* magazine. Believing I had a right to choose my behavior, I asked myself this question: Should I look at this *Playboy* or not?

The moment I asked that question, I opened myself to counsel. I began talking pros and cons to myself. But far worse, I opened myself to Satan's counsel. He wanted to be heard on this issue....

Therein lies the power of temptation. You may fear that temptation will be too strong for you in this battle, but temptations honestly have no power at all without our own arrogant questions. 📖

📖 Looking back at the details of our plan, even we will admit that it all sounds slightly crazy. Defenses, brain tricks, bouncing your eyes, forfeiting rights. Man! We wonder if even Job would be a bit startled.

On the other hand, maybe we should expect a sound plan to look this way. Consider all the men who are called to purity, yet so few seem to know how to do it. 📖

Discussion Questions

E. Which parts of chapter 13 in *Every Man's Battle* were most helpful or encouraging to you and why?

F. Have you ever "been there" at the ice machine with Fred? What did you do in a similar situation?

G. According to Fred, what is the problem with getting into a conversation with ourselves about how we should respond to a particular temptation?

H. Fred and Steve admit that their plan for purity may seem slightly crazy. Have you had that reaction during this course of study? Talk about it!

I. As an additional group-discussion option, look together at the text under the heading The Heart of a Woman at the end of this week's reading. What is most surprising to you in the comments of these women? What is most helpful to you in better understanding your own wife?

victory with your mind

This week's reading assignment:

chapters 14-16 in *Every Man's Battle*

The great news is that the defense perimeter of the eyes works with you to build the perimeter of the mind. The mind needs an object for its lust, so when the eyes view sexual images, the mind has plenty to dance with. Without those images, the mind has an empty dance card. By starving the eyes, you starve the mind as well.

—from chapter 14 in *Every Man's Battle*

EVERY MAN'S TRUTH
(Your Personal Journey into God's Word)

As you begin this week's study, read and meditate upon the following Bible passages, which deal with appreciating God's grace, love, and power. Remember that you can choose to fill your mind with thoughts of God's goodness throughout your day. Think on these things!

> Answer me, O LORD, out of the goodness of your love;
>> in your great mercy turn to me.
> Do not hide your face from your servant;
>> answer me quickly, for I am in trouble.

Come near and rescue me;

redeem me because of my foes.

(Psalm 69:16-18)

Praise be to the God and Father of our Lord Jesus Christ, who has blessed us in the heavenly realms with every spiritual blessing in Christ. For he chose us in him before the creation of the world to be holy and blameless in his sight. In love he predestined us to be adopted as his sons through Jesus Christ, in accordance with his pleasure and will—to the praise of his glorious grace, which he has freely given us in the One he loves. In him we have redemption through his blood, the forgiveness of sins, in accordance with the riches of God's grace that he lavished on us with all wisdom and understanding. (Ephesians 1:3-8)

Finally, brothers, whatever is true, whatever is noble, whatever is right, whatever is pure, whatever is lovely, whatever is admirable—if anything is excellent or praiseworthy—think about such things. (Philippians 4:8)

1. Have you ever prayed the words of Psalm 69 that King David prayed? Do you have this fellow sinner's confidence in God's goodness, love, and mercy?

2. Meditate upon the blessings proclaimed in Ephesians 1:3-8. Make a list of the spiritual riches bestowed upon you as an adopted son of the heavenly Father. How will you live as His son today?

3. To what extent will your mind need transforming if you are to carry out the apostle's command in Philippians 4:8?

✓ Every Man's CHOICE
(Questions for Personal Reflection and Examination)

📖 Your mind is orderly, and your worldview colors what comes through it. The mind will allow impure thoughts only if they "fit" the way you look at the world. As you set up the perimeter of defense for your mind, your brain's worldview will be transformed by a new matrix of allowed thoughts, or "allowables."…

This transformation of the mind takes some time as you wait for the old sexual pollution to be washed away. It's much like living near a creek that becomes polluted when a sewer main breaks upstream. After repair crews replace the cracked sewage pipe, it will still take some time for the water downstream to clear. 📖

📖 Have you "lurked at your neighbor's door"? It could mean stopping by in the late afternoon, visiting your friend's wife for coffee, enamored by her wisdom, care, and sensitivity. You felt sorry for her as you've commiserated together over her insensitive, brutish husband. You held her as she cried. You were lurking at your neighbor's door. 📖

4. Why is the mind more difficult to control than the eyes? How will your eyes work together with your mind in your pursuit of sexual purity?

5. What do the authors mean by "lurking at the door" and "mental lurking"? What is your own experience with this?

👟 EVERY MAN'S WALK
(Your Guide to Personal Application)

📖 According to Jesus, doing it mentally is the same as doing it physically.

📖 Currently, your mind runs like a mustang. What's more, your mind "mates" where it wills with attractive, sensual women. They're everywhere. With a mustang mind, how do you stop the running and the mating? With a corral around your mind. 📖

6. How seriously do you take Jesus' words in Matthew 5:28?

7. How would you explain the authors' corral concept as it applies to sexual purity in your thought life? What does the corral represent, and what does it accomplish?

8. How useful do you think this corral concept can be for you?

9. In quietness, review what you have written and learned in this week's study. If further thoughts or prayer requests come to your mind and heart, you may want to write them here.

🙂🙃 EVERY MAN'S TALK

(Constructive Topics and Questions for Group Discussion)

Key Highlights from the Book for Reading Aloud and Discussing

📖 The defense perimeter of the mind is less like a wall and more like a customs area in an international airport. Customs departments are filters, preventing dangerous elements from entering a country. The U.S. Customs Service attempts to filter out drugs, Mediterranean fruit flies, terrorists, and other harmful agents.

   Similarly, the defense perimeter of the mind properly processes attractive women into your "country," filtering out the alien seeds of attraction before the impure thoughts are even generated. This perimeter "stops the lurking." 📖

📖 Jack: "I knew that kiss would end my career at my church, but I couldn't help myself." 📖

Discussion Questions

A. Which parts of chapter 14 in *Every Man's Battle* were most helpful or encouraging to you and why?

B. How would you explain the process, as explained in this chapter, by which the mind cleans away old sexual pollution? What encouragement does understanding this process give you?

C. What do the authors mean by a "mental customs station"? Describe this process in practical terms.

D. What do the authors mean by "starving the attractions"? What would it mean practically in your life?

E. Recall Fred's story of his high-school crush on Judy—and the disaster prom date that ended it. Fred said: "My attractions to Judy died that night. The facts did them in!" Discuss the problem of filling in the blanks versus letting the facts do their attraction-reducing work.

Note: If you're following a twelve-week track,
save the rest of this lesson for the following week.
If you're on the eight-week track...then keep going.

☑ EVERY MAN'S CHOICE
(Questions for Personal Reflection and Examination)

📖 Think about two types of women who will approach your corral:

- Women you find attractive;
- Women who find you attractive.

Both categories have similar defenses, each designed to starve the attractions until she trots off toward the horizon. 📖

10. What are the most important principles for having effective defenses against impure thoughts regarding women you find attractive?

11. What are the most important principles for having effective defenses against impure thoughts regarding women who find you attractive?

12. What is your level of temptation toward old girlfriends and/or ex-wives? wives of friends? What are the authors' most helpful suggestions to you in these areas?

👟 EVERY MAN'S WALK
(Your Guide to Personal Application)

> 📖 Always play the dweeb. Players flirt.... Learn to un-flirt. Players banter.... Learn to un-banter. If a woman smiles with a knowing look, learn to smile with a slightly confused look, to un-smile. If she talks about things that are hip, talk about things that are un-hip to her, like your wife and kids. She'll find you pleasant enough but rather bland and uninteresting. Perfect. 📖

> 📖 It's not that you don't trust your friend's wife; it's that you don't want to start anything. She should be like a sister to you, with no hint of attraction between you.
>
> You'll always have some relationship with your friend's wife, but limit it to when your friend is around. This isn't

always possible, but some simple rules can shield you from surprise attacks within the corral. 📖

13. Review the four "shields" from surprise attacks related to friends' wives. Consider the practicality of each suggestion for your own life.

14. What do the authors mean by "playing the dweeb," and how effective do you think this tactic can be in your own life?

15. In your own life, what do you believe are the most important factors that will ensure the success of the authors' entire strategy for purity (that is, bouncing, starving, corralling, playing the dweeb, and so on)?

16. a) What for you was the most meaningful concept or truth in this week's study?

b) How would you talk this over with God? Write your response here as a prayer to Him.

c) What do you believe God wants you to do in response to this week's study?

👥 EVERY MAN'S TALK
(More Topics and Questions for Group Discussion)

Key Highlights from the Book for Reading Aloud and Discussing

📖 For those women who are already within your corral, the situation becomes rather complicated. These women won't drift back to the horizon. They're in your corral today and probably will be there tomorrow and the next day. This means you must eliminate these attractions in some other way. Let's take a look at the two main categories of women within your corral: old girlfriends and ex-wives; wives of your friends. 📖

📖 In *The Final Quest*, Rick Joyner writes, "Spiritual maturity is always dictated by our willingness to sacrifice our own desires for the desires of others or for the interests of the kingdom."

Purifying your eyes and mind is more than a command—it's also a sacrifice. And as you make that sacrifice, as you lay down your desires, blessings will flow. Your spiritual life will experience new joy and power, and your marriage life will blossom as your relationship reaches new heights.

Discussion Questions

F. Which parts of chapters 15 and 16 in *Every Man's Battle* were most helpful or encouraging to you and why?

G. What tactics were presented for maintaining pure thoughts in regard to old girlfriends and ex-wives? What is your opinion of their effectiveness?

H. What tactics were presented for maintaining pure thoughts in regard to the wives of your friends? Why is it important to think through this strategy? (Spend several minutes talking about the practical implications for your group.)

I. As an additional group-discussion option, look together at the text under the heading The Heart of a Woman at the end of this week's reading. What is most surprising to you in the comments of these women? What is most helpful to you in better understanding your own wife?

victory in your heart

This week's reading assignment:

chapters 17-18 in *Every Man's Battle*

Let's talk about your innermost perimeter, which is about being consumed with God's purpose to cherish your wife. If Christians were consumed by God's purposes, it would first be reflected in our marriages. But the rates of divorce, adultery, and marital dissatisfaction in the Christian church reveal our hearts. We've known very few men consumed by their marriages, and fewer still consumed by purity, but both are God's desire for you. God's purpose for your marriage is that it parallels Christ's relationship to His church, that you be one with your wife.

—from chapter 17 in *Every Man's Battle*

 EVERY MAN'S TRUTH
(Your Personal Journey into God's Word)

As you begin this final study, take some time to read and meditate upon the following Bible passage, which has to do with the beauty of the bride—the bride of Christ and also your own bride. Keep in mind that, for centuries, the Song of Solomon has often been viewed as an allegory of how Christ feels for His bride (all believers).

> How beautiful you are, my darling!
>> Oh, how beautiful!
>> Your eyes behind your veil are doves....
> Your lips are like a scarlet ribbon;
>> Your mouth is lovely....
> All beautiful you are, my darling;
>> there is no flaw in you....
> You have stolen my heart, my sister, my bride;
>> you have stolen my heart
> with one glance of your eyes....
> How delightful is your love, my sister, my bride!...
> Your head crowns you like Mount Carmel.
>> Your hair is like royal tapestry;
>> the king is held captive by its tresses.
> How beautiful you are and how pleasing,
>> O love, with your delights!
>> (Song of Songs 4:1,3,7,9-10; 7:5-6)

1. Do you sense Jesus' desire for you as part of His bride? In return, does your heart yearn for Him like this?

2. Because our marriage relationships should parallel Christ's relationship to the church, our feelings for our wives should parallel these passages. Can you be content with the wife of your youth? (If she isn't all you'd hoped for, remember that God graced you with this ewe lamb.)

3. Can you make a commitment to cherish her today?

☑ EVERY MAN'S CHOICE
(Questions for Personal Reflection and Examination)

📖 Are you cherishing your wife? Do you feel cherished?

If not, you probably got there the same way I did— by stopping short of God's standards. God's standard is to unconditionally cherish her, no matter what. No conditions. But in America, we've added mealy-mouthed terms to form "conditional contracts."…The problem comes when we expect our wives to deliver these things under contractual conditions. With Brenda, anger and resentment erupted when I felt she didn't carry her side of the bargain. I no longer felt like cherishing her. 📖

4. Review carefully the teaching in Ephesians 5:25-33 in light of all you've learned in this book and your study during the previous weeks. Why do you think so many husbands tend to resist the teaching of this passage?

5. State in your own words what this passage teaches in regard to your marriage and Christ's relationship to the church. What are the right attitudes and convictions as taught in this passage? What are the right standards and ideals? What are the right actions and habits?

6. What does it really mean to you to cherish your wife?

7. What contractual conditions have you been trying to hold your wife to over the years? Were you consciously aware of doing this? What now needs to change?

📖 EVERY MAN'S WALK
(Your Guide to Personal Application)

📖 Your wife gave up her freedom for you. She relinquished her rights to seek happiness elsewhere. She exchanged this freedom for something she considered more valuable: your love and your word. Her dreams are tied up in you, dreams of sharing and communication and oneness.

She's pledged to be yours sexually. Her sexuality is her most guarded possession, her secret garden. She trusted you would be worthy of this gift, but you have cavalierly viewed sensual garbage, polluting and littering her garden. She deserves more, and you must honor that. 📖

📖 In my office I keep an eight-by-ten, black-and-white photo of Brenda when she was one year old. Her little eyes sparkle and are filled with the hope and joy of life, her mischievous smile apparent even then; her glowing, chubby cheeks radiating joy and a carefree spirit. That face is so full of expectations and wonder. I brought that infant picture to my office because it reminds me that I need to honor that hope. 📖

8. What has your wife given up for you? What are the most important things your wife has given to you?

9. What are the most important honor issues involved in your marriage? What are the most important ways you can build up and honor your wife's hope?

10. What can you do today to more faithfully honor your wife? What can you do tomorrow? What can you do as a new habit for the rest of your life together?

11. In quietness, review what you have written and learned in this week's study. If further thoughts or prayer requests come to your mind and heart, you may want to write them here.

12. a) What for you was the most meaningful concept or truth in this week's study?

b) How would you talk this over with God? Write your response here as a prayer to Him.

c) What do you believe God wants you to do in response to this week's study?

👥 EVERY MAN'S TALK
(Constructive Topics and Questions for Group Discussion)

Key Highlights from the Book for Reading Aloud and Discussing

📖 What does the standard of Christ's relationship to His church have to do with our sexual purity? In our hearts, we often have selfish attitudes and expectations regarding our wives. When these expectations aren't met, we become grumpy and frustrated. Our will to maintain our outer defense perimeters is eroded. Well, if this is how she's going to be, why should I go through all the effort of being pure? She doesn't deserve it. We retaliate by withdrawing from our own responsibilities. 📖

📖 Uriah knew his place. He was satisfied to be part of God's purposes, to fill his role. To be like Uriah, we must know our place and be content with it. 📖

📖 In our society, we have "sensitivity training" and "cross-cultural enrichment" classes. We believe if we can only teach people the "right" feelings, they'll act correctly. In the Bible, however, God tells us the opposite: We're to first act correctly, and then right feelings will follow.

If you don't feel like cherishing, cherish anyway. Your right feelings will arrive soon enough. 📖

Discussion Questions

A. Which parts of chapters 17 and 18 in *Every Man's Battle* were most helpful or encouraging to you and why?

B. When have you been grumpy and frustrated when your expectations for your wife haven't been met? Can you share about a recent example? How do you typically retaliate for unmet expectations?

C. Under the heading How Cherishing Feels in chapter 17, look at the authors' paraphrases from the Song of Solomon. How would you analyze the feelings conveyed in these passages? How helpful are these passages as tools for understanding your proper emotional involvement with your wife?

D. Look at the quotation above about Uriah and then review the story of David, Bathsheba, Uriah, and Nathan (from 2 Samuel 11–12) as summarized by the authors. This is probably a story you've read before. As you consider it again, what stands out to you, now that you've carefully studied sexual purity and made a commitment to pursue it? What are the most important lessons this story has for Christian men today in their marriages?

E. Do you agree that we're to first act correctly and then right feelings will follow? Why or why not? What is your evidence?

F. Take a moment to reflect on what you've studied and discussed during the previous weeks. Ask each man to comment on one or more of these questions:

1. What can you thank God for as a result of this study?

2. What do you sense that God most wants you to understand at this time about this topic?

3. In what specific ways do you believe He wants you now to more fully trust and obey Him?

don't keep it to yourself

If you've just completed the *Every Man's Battle Workbook* on your own, and you found it to be a helpful and valuable experience, we encourage you to consider gathering a group of other men and helping lead them through this workbook together.

You'll find more information about starting such a group on page 2, in the last item under the section called Questions You May Have About This Workbook.

_____

Steve can be reached by e-mail at sarterburn@newlife.com.

Fred can be reached by e-mail at stoekef@qwest.net.

_____

every man's battle workshop

from New Life Ministries

new Life Ministries receives hundreds of calls every month from Christian men who are struggling to stay pure in the midst of daily challenges to their sexual integrity. We are committed to helping men win this battle for sexual purity.

In our Every Man's Battle Workshops, we offer a biblically based program for men who are seeking God's wisdom for keeping themselves pure. In four days of teaching and group counseling, participants gear up for battle as they learn a practical, no-nonsense approach for overcoming the destructive effects of sexual temptation. Our goal is to equip each man who attends with the tools necessary to maintain sexual integrity and enjoy healthy, productive relationships.

The topics covered in this Christ-centered environment include:
- the nature of sexual temptation
- false intimacy
- boundaries
- trust and communication in marriage
- temptation cycles and how to manage them
- emotional conflicts
- the daily disciplines

Please call 1-800-NEW-LIFE

to speak with one of our specialists
about the next Every Man's Battle Workshop.